This is Why You're Broke

Break the Cycle. Build the Legacy. Live with Peace

Author/Editor: Rev. Darryl Bass

Electronic ISBN: 978-1-972115-06-0 (EPUB)
                  978-1-972115-35-0 (Kindle)
Paperback ISBN: 978-1-972115-08-4
Hardcover ISBN: 978-1-972115-07-7
Printed in the United States

The Library of Congress Control Number: 2026906642

Bass Publishing, LLC
Maywood, IL 60153

Disclaimer

The information contained in this book is for educational and informational purposes only. It is not intended as financial, legal, tax, medical, psychological, or professional advice. The author and publisher make no guarantees regarding the results that may be obtained from the use of this material.

All examples provided are illustrative and are not intended to represent or guarantee that any individual will achieve similar results. Personal growth, financial improvement, and life progression outcomes depend on individual effort, discipline, decisions, and circumstances.

Readers are encouraged to seek qualified professional advice regarding financial planning, legal matters, mental health, or other specialized areas before making decisions based on the information provided in this book.

The author and publisher disclaim any liability for any loss, risk, or damages, direct or indirect, that may arise from the use or application of the information contained herein.

By reading this book, you acknowledge that you are responsible for your own decisions, actions, and results.

Details in any stories and anecdotes have been changed to protect the identities of the person(s) involved.

DEDICATION

This book is dedicated to **my children**, and to every child who will one day carry our family name.

May you never have to recover from financial stress, rebuild from instability, or learn survival the hard way.
May peace be your foundation, wisdom be your inheritance, and opportunity be your normal.
I changed so you wouldn't have to start where I started.

And this book is also dedicated to **every person who is tired.**
Tired of struggling.
Tired of starting over.
Tired of looking strong while feeling overwhelmed inside.
Tired of pretending they're okay when life has been heavy.

To you, I say this:

There is nothing wrong with you.
You are not behind.
You are not broken.
You are not weak.
You are *becoming.*

You are the turning point in your family.
You are the one who breaks the cycle.
You are the one who brings the shift.
You are the one who changes everything.

This book is your permission to begin again.
This time — with clarity, dignity, and peace.

You were always meant to rise.
And your rise begins now.

— Rev. Darryl Bass

FOREWORD

There comes a moment when survival is no longer enough. A moment when juggling bills, stretching paychecks, and pretending everything is fine becomes heavier than the fear of change. That moment is not weakness. It is awakening.

This book was not written to shame you. It was written to free you.

For many of us, hard work was taught — but structure was not. We learned how to earn, but not how to build. We learned how to survive, but not how to create peace. Over time, habits formed. Patterns repeated. And without realizing it, we inherited financial cycles we never chose consciously.

This Is Why You're Broke does not attack your character. It challenges your habits. It does not condemn your past. It clarifies your future.

Rev. Darryl Bass speaks with both compassion and clarity. His message is direct because the stakes are real. Financial struggle is rarely about laziness or intelligence. It is about identity, discipline, mindset, and decisions that were never examined.

But this book does more than raise awareness. It offers structure. It calls for intentional budgeting, disciplined spending, wise protection, increased income, and long-term legacy thinking. It reminds you that peace is built — not wished for.

Beneath the financial instruction lies something deeper: dignity.

This is about becoming the turning point in your family.
This is about ending cycles instead of explaining them.
This is about building something that lasts.

The struggle does not define you.
Your decision does.

And that decision begins now.

Contents

INTRODUCTION

Let's have a real conversation.
Not the kind where we pretend everything is fine
while our accounts sitting on "hope and a prayer."
No, I mean an honest one. The kind that makes
you shift in your chair a little.

Because the truth is:
**Most of us aren't broke because life is unfair.
We're broke because we've developed habits
that disrespect our future.**

And I say that with love.

I have sat across kitchen tables, church pews,
office desks, and restaurant booths with people
whose hearts were full of dreams — but whose
wallets were full of chaos. And I realized
something:

Money is rarely the real problem.
It's the mindset behind the money.

1

See, being "broke" is not the absence of money.
Being broke is the condition of always having
plans bigger than your paycheck because your
paycheck is already spoken for by bills, debt, old
decisions, and emotional spending.

Some of us are not just broke.
Some of us are *broke, tired, overwhelmed, behind,
stressed, and praying nobody brings up that money we owe.*

This book is not here to judge you.
This book is not here to shame you.

This book is here to **wake you up**.

Because you deserve more than:

Working every month just to stay afloat

Stressing over due dates

Rearranging bills like puzzle pieces

Pretending you're okay while you're silently
drowning

You deserve:

Peace

Options

Stability

Overflow
and most importantly —
A financial life that matches your purpose.

Let me tell you something I deeply believe:

God never designed you to live in financial captivity.
Not emotionally.
Not spiritually.
Not economically.

But freedom is never accidental.
It is intentional.
It is structured.
It is practiced.

This book is your roadmap back to yourself.

Over the next chapters, we're going to confront:

Your rent

Your car choices

Your spending patterns

Your debt

Your food habits

Your circle

Your upgrades

Your lack of margin

Your income strategy

Your financial identity

Not with guilt.
But with clarity.

And clarity **changes everything**.

What I Need from You

Not perfection.
Not overnight miracles.
Just honesty.
And a willingness to do something different this time — not for the bill collectors, not for social media, not for your friends…

…but for your future self.

Because they're depending on you.

CHAPTER 1: WHEN THE RENT EATS FIRST, YOUR FUTURE EATS LAST

Let me tell you a moment I have seen more times than I can count.

You're sitting at the kitchen table with your paycheck in one hand and your bills in the other. You already know the math ain't mathing. You haven't even *started* writing numbers down and somehow the money already feels gone.

Rent hits first.
And once that rent hits?
You already know what kind of month it's about to be.

You're not thinking about savings.
You're not thinking about debt.
You're not thinking about investing.
You're thinking:

"How do I survive the next 27 days without losing my mind?"

And let's be real — some of us ain't just surviving the month...
we're surviving the week.

See, the problem for many of us is not that we don't make money.
It's that our money is **already living somewhere else** before we even touch it.

Rent is taking up **way too much space in our financial lives.**

And nobody told us that the number we chose for rent was the first domino that determines:

Whether we stress or breathe

Whether we build or borrow

Whether we move forward or stay stuck

But today, you gon' hear it plain:

**If your rent is eating more than 30–35% of
your income, your future is starving.**

And most of us?
We feeding rent like we owe it our loyalty.

Let's Talk Facts

We tell ourselves:

"I deserve a nice place."

"I deserve peace of mind."

"I can't just live anywhere."

And listen —
You do deserve peace.
You do deserve comfort.
You do deserve safety.

But when your peace comes with:

stress every payday,

panic every bill cycle,

and silence when the group chat asks, "Who's going?"

…that's not peace.
That's **financial anxiety with hardwood floors.**

Here's the Truth We Don't Like To Say Out Loud

You can't afford "peace of mind" when the cost of your peace is your **progress.**

You can't claim "I'm grown, I got my own place" if the cost of having your own place is:

No savings

No emergency fund

No debt payoff

No investments

No margin

No options

That's not independence.
That's just **expensive pride.**

And pride has late fees.

Let's Call It What It Is

If rent is:

Half your income,

60% of your income,

70% of your income…

Then you're working every month to **pay to exist**, not to live.
And survival was never your calling.

You were meant for:

Ownership

Legacy

Generational stability

Wealth that outlives you

But we can't build a future while fighting every month to stay afloat today.

So Here's the Shift

This chapter isn't asking you to downsize forever. It's asking you to **reposition temporarily** so you can **elevate permanently.**

There is no shame in:

Roommates for a season

Moving back home to rebuild

Relocating strategically

Committing to a short-term sacrifice to gain long-term freedom

Because hear me:

You don't have to live small forever — but you will have to think smarter today.

Freedom is built in steps.
Peace is built in planning.
Legacy is built in discipline.

And the first move toward your financial future is simple:

Get your rent under control.
Your future depends on it.

Before We Turn the Page

Take a breath.

Now answer honestly — just to yourself:

If your future self were watching you today, would they thank you for your current decisions... or ask you why you wasted so much time?

That answer is the start of your transformation.

CHAPTER 2 — YOUR CAR IS DISRESPECTING YOUR PAYCHECK

Let's talk about that car.

You know the one.

The one that looked good sitting on the dealership floor with the lights shining on it like it was God-sent and *chosen just for you.*

The one that had that new car smell that made you feel like life finally turned a corner.

The one you said,

"I work hard — I deserve this."

And listen — I'm not here to tell you, you don't deserve nice things. You do. But, deserving something and **being positioned for it** are not the same thing.

14

Because here's the moment most of us realized
something wasn't adding up:

You got that car…
That first payment hit…
Then the insurance quote came in…
Then the gas tank laughed at you…

And suddenly that car wasn't a blessing — it was
a **bill on wheels.**

Let Me Paint the Real Scene

You pull up somewhere looking good.
Music bumping.
Windows clean.
New tires.
Fresh wash.

But the whole time your heart is beating at the
speed of the repo truck you hope never comes
around the corner.

You smiling…
But your checking account is whispering:

"This ain't sustainable."

And your spirit is whispering:

"We did this for *who* and for *what?*"

See, most of us didn't buy a car…
We bought **validation.**

We bought:

Approval

Confidence

Identity

A "statement"

But statements don't build wealth.
Statements build stress.

The Real Cost of That Car

You may think your car costs:

$450 a month

But that's just the *note*.

Let's talk real numbers:

Expense	Monthly Reality
Car Note	$400–$700
Insurance	$120–$260
Gas	$140–$240
Repairs & Maintenance	$60–$150
Depreciation (Value drops)	$100–$250

Total: $820–$1,600 a month
on something that loses value every day you drive it.

That's not transportation.
That's a **financial slow leak.**

And many people are losing thousands every year
and calling it "the standard."

Let Me Say This Clearly

If your car is eating the money your future needs
to grow…
If your car note is stopping you from building
savings…
If your car payment is louder than your peace…

That car is not a blessing.
It's bondage — dressed in leather seats.

You Don't Need a Luxury Car to Have a Luxury Life

The most financially stable families you'll ever meet are driving:

Hondas

Toyotas

Nissans

A reliable used car that starts *every time they turn the key*

Why?

Because wealth is not shown in **what you drive.** Wealth is shown in **what you can afford not to worry about.**

Freedom > Flexing.
Stability > Status.
Peace > Perception.

So Here's How You Get Your Power Back

This isn't about pride.
This is about positioning.

Rule:

Buy a car you can pay off quickly — or buy it in cash.

Older is okay.

Reliable is the goal.

Paid off is the blessing.

If the car you drive today costs you your ability to save, invest, breathe, and move — then the car is not serving your life... **you are serving the car.**

And you weren't built to serve *anything* that was supposed to serve *you*.

Let Me Free You from Something

There is no shame in:

Downsizing

Trading that car in

Selling it

Starting temporary so you can finish permanent

Temporary sacrifice is not loss — it is strategy.

And strategy is how wealth is built.

Ask Yourself This:

If nobody could *see* what you drive...
If nobody could *comment* on it...
If nobody knew the brand, the year, the model...

Would you still want the same car?

If the answer is no...

Then you didn't buy the car for *you*.

And now we fix that.

CHAPTER 3 — DEBT IS NOT JUST MONEY. IT'S A MINDSET.

Let me tell you about a moment I've seen a thousand times.

You're sitting there, phone in hand, scrolling casually…
Then you see that notification:

"Payment Due."

Not *"Paid."*
Not *"Available Balance."*

Just **Due** — like a bill collector got the nerve to call you by your first name.

And suddenly, everything in your spirit just gets tired.

Not frustrated.
Not irritated.
Tired.

Tired of working so hard just to stay in the same place.
Tired of owing.
Tired of juggling.
Tired of managing stress disguised as "normal life."

And for a moment — even if you don't say it out loud — the truth rises up:

I'm tired of being controlled by debt.

But here's the part that stings:

Most of us **didn't get into debt because we didn't have money.**
We got into debt because we wanted life to move faster than our discipline was willing to grow.

Let that breathe.

Debt Isn't Just a Financial Issue

Debt is emotional.
Debt is psychological.
Debt is spiritual.
Debt is cultural.
Debt is learned.

Most of us didn't wake up one day and say:
"Let me go destroy my peace today."

No.
Debt creeps in.

Debt starts with:

"I'll pay it back later."

"This is just for now."

"I work hard, I deserve this."

"It's only $25/month."

"I'll catch up next check."

Debt is built one compromise at a time.

25

And if nobody ever taught us how to handle money, the world gladly taught us instead.

But the world taught us how to **spend**, not how to **keep**.

Debt Has a Personality

Debt is loud.
Debt is demanding.
Debt is never satisfied.
Debt will interrupt your life like it owns you.

It talks like this:

"Oh, you got a raise? Let me hold that."

"Oh, you finally caught up? Let me remind you what you owe."

"Oh, you thought you were free? Not yet."

Debt doesn't just take money.
It takes hope.

It takes sleep.
It takes confidence.

Debt destroys dreams.

Debt mutilates momentum.

Debt steals future blessings and makes you pay
for yesterday's decisions with tomorrow's income.

Debt Happens When Your Future Self Stops Having a Voice

Every time we used a credit card, we were
borrowing from our future.

Every time we financed something we couldn't
afford, we were telling our future:

"You handle it. I'll enjoy it now."

But your future self is tired of handling what your
past self didn't want to be patient for.

This is bigger than math.

This is maturity.

Let's Be Clear:

Getting out of debt is not about shame.
It's about **strategy**.

This is the moment when you say:

"I'm not living like this anymore."

Not because debt is evil.
Not because spending is sinful.
Not because you don't deserve nice things.

But because:
**You deserve to experience life without stress
screaming in your ear.**

You deserve:

Days without panic

Paychecks that stay yours

Money that grows instead of disappears

Freedom to make decisions without fear

Debt is loud.
But **your future self needs to be louder.**

And Here's the Good News

Debt can be defeated.
Not in theory — in real life.

It doesn't matter:

How much you make now

How long you've been struggling

How many mistakes you've made

I've seen people with $60,000 in debt wipe it out
in under 2 years.
I've seen families who were drowning go on to

build wealth.
I've seen people with credit scores in the 400s buy homes in cash.

Not because they were special.
Because they got **fed up and focused.**

Debt is not permanent.
Your story is not fixed.
Your situation is not final.

But it *will* require change.
And sacrifice.
And honesty.
And consistency.

And you are strong enough for all of that.

So Here's Your First Declaration:

Say this out loud — slowly:

I do not work to pay debt.
I work to build my future.

I do not work to survive.
I work to create legacy.

Debt is not my identity.
Freedom is.

Again:

I do not work to pay debt.
I work to build my future.

I do not work to survive.
I work to create legacy.

Debt is not my identity.
Freedom is.

One more time with meaning:

I do not work to pay debt.
I work to build my future.

I do not work to survive.
I work to create legacy.

**Debt is not my identity.
Freedom is.**

Now let it settle.

CHAPTER 4 — YOUR FOOD SPENDING IS EATING YOUR FUTURE

Let me paint a moment we've all lived:

You tell yourself, *"I'm not eating out this week."*
You said it with your chest.
You meant it.

Then life lifed you.

Now it's lunchtime.
You're tired.
Your morning was heavy.
You didn't meal prep.
And that little voice whispers:

"It's just $12…"

But it's never *just* $12.

Because tomorrow, you're tired again.
The next day, you forgot again.
Friday feels like "I deserve this."
Saturday becomes "I don't feel like cooking."
Sunday turns into brunch — where we spend like
rent is already paid and our destiny is on autopay.

And now, instead of $12...
You've spent **$180 this week** on *food you barely
remember eating.*

Not because you're irresponsible.
But because you were **unaware.**

Food spending is the quiet thief.

It doesn't feel reckless.
It doesn't look wild.
It feels... normal.

But "normal" is exactly what keeps so many of us
stuck.

Let's Break Down What's Really Happening

Food spending is emotional.
We eat when we're:

Bored

Overwhelmed

Celebrating

Worn down

Trying to feel better

Trying to feel *something*

Food isn't just food.
Food is comfort.
Food is reward.
Food is escape.

So the problem is not the food.
The problem is the moment.

The moment where eating gave us a break —
that's what we're really paying for.

But peace shouldn't cost $600 a month.

And Then There's Groceries

Let's talk about that grocery cart.

You walked into the store thinking you were
going to spend $50.
Next thing you know — it's $137.42.

Why?

Because we shop like we cook five-course meals
every night…
when really we rotate the same three foods
anyway.

We are **buying groceries to feel productive,
not to actually eat with intention.**

Groceries without a plan = food that spoils
Spoiled food = wasted money
Wasted money = guilt
Guilt = more emotional eating
More emotional eating = more spending

And the cycle continues.

This Is Not About Shame. It's About Awareness.

If you eat out 5 days a week at $15 a meal:

That's **$75 a week**
...which is **$300 a month**
...which is **$3,600 a year.**

Now add:

Weekend food runs

Snacks

Coffee stops

DoorDash

"I didn't feel like cooking" moments

Now we're looking at **$5,800 – $8,200 a year** on food that never built your future — just fed the moment.

And that's money that could have:

Built your 3-month emergency fund

Paid down your debt

Started you investing

Covered insurance

Built savings

Opened the door to breathing room

But instead of seed, it became **seasoning.**

Here's the Shift

We are not dieting.
We are **disciplining.**

We are not restricting.
We are **restructuring.**

We are not cutting food.
We are **cutting mindless food.**

Because **you deserve to feel full — not financially emptied.**

Here's the Practical Plan

To get food spending under control, do this:

Groceries — Set a *monthly* number.
Example: $120–$180 (single), $300–$500 (family)

Daily Eating Out Limit
Give yourself a *per day* amount.
Example:
Weekdays: $6–$8
Weekends: $10–$14

Amusement Eating (Brunch, Dates, Uber Eats)
Give this **one number per month**.
Example: $40–$75

This turns food from **impulsive** to **intentional.**

You still get to enjoy life — but now **your future gets to enjoy it too.**

And Say This to Yourself:

I will not keep feeding my stress while starving my future.

Because you were never meant to live just making it.

You were built for overflow — but overflow requires order.

And order always begins at the table.

CHAPTER 5 — YOUR CLOTHES ARE NICE, BUT YOUR FUTURE IS NAKED

Here's a moment we don't talk about enough:

You're getting dressed to go somewhere —
maybe a party, church event, gathering, brunch, or
just stepping out because you needed air.

You're in the mirror, laying out the fit.
You got the shoes, the jacket, the accessories, the
smell-good.
And you're looking right.
Clean. Pulled together. Sharp.

But while you're admiring how good the *outside*
looks...

There's a quiet voice inside that says:

"If only my bank account looked as good as I do
right now."

41

That's when it hits.

We've learned to **dress the version of ourselves we want the world to see...**
even when that version does not match what's really happening in our finances.

And hear me clearly:

There's nothing wrong with wanting to look good.
There's nothing wrong with excellence, presentation, style, or expression.

But there *is* something wrong when:

We look expensive, but live stressed

We dress confident, but feel financially insecure

We buy outfits, hoping they fix how we feel inside

That's not fashion.
That's **financial performance.**

And it's costing us — quietly.

We Don't Buy Clothes — We Buy Identity

When we purchase clothes beyond our budget, we are usually buying:

Confidence

Validation

A sense of belonging

Proof that we're "doing okay"

A moment of escape from responsibility

We're not buying shirts.
We're buying **a version of ourselves we haven't grown into yet.**

The problem is — when your spending is rooted in identity, you keep needing *more* to feel the same effect.

And that's how you end up with:

43

A closet full of clothes

But a life full of financial pressure

That's not God's design.
That's culture's influence.

Let's Be Even More Honest

Some of us are not buying clothes because we want them…

We're buying clothes because somewhere inside, we don't feel **enough** without them.

Read that again.

If you need:

The outfit…

The jewelry…

The nails…

44

The bag…

The shoes…

…in order to **feel like yourself** — then something deeper needs healing that no designer, logo, or fit can fix.

Your identity is not hanging in your closet.

The Real Flex

You know what confidence sounds like?

"I don't need to prove anything to anybody."

"I'm good whether I'm dressed up or in a basic tee."

"I look like me — not like a price tag."

"My future is more expensive than this outfit."

The real flex is:

Paid bills

Growing savings

No credit card balances

Real investments

Money that stays in your pocket

The real flex is:
Peace.

So Let's Shift the Strategy

We're not saying:

Don't look good

Don't have style

Don't enjoy clothes

No. We're saying:

**Buy fewer things — but buy better quality.
And keep it long enough for it to be worth it.**

46

Here's the rule:

If you don't *love* it — don't buy it.

If it's not in the budget — don't buy it.

If it's only for the picture — don't buy it.

If you're only buying it because you saw someone else wearing it — don't buy it.

If you already have something like it — don't buy it.

Clothes should **serve your life**, not derail your progress.

Style Isn't What You Wear.

Style is:

How you carry yourself

How you speak

How you treat people

How you handle business

How you present your character, not just your outfit

Anyone can buy clothes.
Not everyone can build identity.

And identity is what we're cultivating here.

Say This to Yourself:

I don't dress to impress strangers.
I dress to honor who I am becoming.

Because the version of you that is building:

Legacy

Wealth

Peace

Freedom

Stability

Confidence

...doesn't need anybody's approval to walk in the room.

You carry your value — it does not hang in your closet.

CHAPTER 6 — SOME OF YOUR FRIENDS ARE TOO EXPENSIVE

Let's talk about the people around you.

Not the people who *love* you.
Not the people who *push* you.
Not the people who want to see you win.

No — the *other ones*.

The ones where every time you start getting serious about your money, your goals, your peace, your discipline…

Here they come with:

The invites

The pressure

The "come on, live a little"

The "you acting brand new"

And you start feeling bad for wanting better.

Let's call it what it is:

Some friendships are costing you your future.

Not because they're bad people.
Not because they're evil.
Not because they want to see you fail.

But because **they are comfortable where you are trying to leave.**

And staying connected **the same way** keeps you tied to a version of yourself you are trying to outgrow.

You Were Not Meant to Outgrow People — But You *Will* Outgrow Patterns

Read that again slowly.

51

Your elevation is not a rejection of them.
It is a commitment to you.

But here's the hard truth:

A lot of people love you **as long as you stay
who they know.**
The moment you start changing?
They get uncomfortable.

Not because your change is wrong.
But because your change reminds them of what
they're not changing.

And some people will sabotage your growth just
to protect their comfort.

Your Circle Is Either Fuel or Weight

There are only two kinds of people in your life:

1. People who multiply you
Who speak life, discipline, push, prayer,
accountability, vision, and elevation.

2. People who drain you
Who require energy just to maintain the
relationship.

You know the difference by how you feel after
interacting with them.

If after spending time with someone you feel:

Tired

Drained

Distracted

Unfocused

Broke

Less confident

Less disciplined

That's not friendship.
That's **emotional expense.**

And you cannot build wealth while paying for someone else's comfort with your peace.

Let's Be Even More Honest

Some of your "fun friends" are really:

Avoidance partners

Chaos buddies

Distraction companions

Y'all not bonding —
Y'all running from the same problems in different ways.

And every time you try to change, they remind you of who you *used* to be.

But hear this:

You cannot grow in an environment that keeps pulling you back into who you're trying to heal from.

This Is Not About Cutting People Off

That's the easy part.

This is about **redefining how the relationship functions.**

Here's how:

Reduce the time spent — don't break the bond.

Shift the conversations — don't carry their emotional weight.

Meet in controlled spaces — not in environments that trigger bad habits.

Be clear about your goals — so they know the new rules.

If someone gets offended because you're trying to improve your life —

55

they were *never celebrating you.*
They were celebrating your *stagnation.*

And Let's Talk About Lending Money

Stop.
Just stop.

If they are always:

Short

Behind

"Trying to figure it out"

Needing "a little something till Friday"

But never changing the *behavior* that caused the
shortage…

You are not helping.
You are **funding their cycle.**

Do not finance someone's unwillingness to grow.

Love them, yes.
Pray for them, absolutely.
But **stop rescuing people who have no
intention of leaving the fire.**

Say This:

**My destiny is too expensive to be discounted
for comfort.**

I will not apologize for growing.

**I am allowed to become better than where I
started.**

And anyone who loves you — truly loves you —
will cheer for your growth.

Even if it challenges them.

CHAPTER 7 — YOUR CHILDREN ARE WATCHING YOUR FINANCIAL HABITS

Here's a moment that hits different:

You're standing in the store with your child.
They see something they want — a snack, a toy, a shirt, shoes, something small.
And they look up at you with hope in their eyes.

And you feel that sting in your chest because you *want* to say yes.
But your account already said no.

So you say the famous line:

"We don't have money for that right now."

But the truth isn't just that we don't have the money.

The truth is:

We never learned how to manage the money we did have.

And without meaning to…
we begin passing down **the same patterns** we're trying to outgrow.

Children Don't Learn Money from What We Say.

They learn it from:

What we *do*

What we *prioritize*

What we *avoid*

What we *stress over*

What we *normalize*

Kids are studying us:

They see:

How we react when bills come

How we treat payday

How we handle desires versus discipline

How we talk about money when we're frustrated

How often we give up our peace for a "moment"

Your child doesn't need you to be perfect.
They just need you to be **aware.**

Because Let's Be Honest

Some of us grew up in homes where money was:

A fight every month

A secret

A stress point

A source of shame

And we were never taught:

How to save

How to budget

How to invest

How to build credit responsibly

How to position ourselves

We were just taught:
"Make it. Spend it. Survive."

But survival isn't the legacy we're building
anymore.

If You Don't Heal Your Financial Patterns, Your Children Will Repeat Them

Children inherit:

Spending habits

Emotional coping habits

Generational beliefs about money

Fear around finances

Avoidance responses to stress

If all they ever see is:

Scrambling

Stressing

"I'll deal with it later"

"I hope it works out"

Then they'll repeat that.

Not because they're weak.
But because **you were their teacher.**

But here's the grace:
This is your chance to rewrite the script.

Your Children Don't Need You to Buy Them More

They need you to:

Show them structure

Model discipline

Teach patience

Demonstrate priorities

Explain WHY you're changing

Let them see consistency

Because **security feels better to a child than toys ever will.**

Stability is love.
Structure is love.
Consistency is love.

The greatest gift you can give your children is not:

Jordans

Tablets

Trips

Clothes

Gadgets

The greatest gift is:
**A childhood that didn't have to recover from
financial instability.**

Here's How You Break the Cycle

Start teaching them:

The difference between *need* and *want*

How to save part of every dollar they receive

That waiting is not denial, it's discipline

That money is a tool — not a master

That their identity is not attached to what they
wear or have

Make money a conversation — not a crisis.

Let them see you:

Pay bills on time

Save intentionally

Say no with confidence

Create plans and stick to them

You don't have to say,
"I'm doing this for you."

They will **feel it**.

Say This Out Loud:

**My children will not have to heal from
financial instability.
They will inherit knowledge, stability, and
opportunity.**

It starts with me. And I am capable.

CHAPTER 8 — IT'S NOT THAT BUDGETING DOESN'T WORK. IT'S THAT WE DON'T FOLLOW ONE.

Let's keep it real.

Most of us don't have a **money problem** — we have a **structure problem**.

We don't budget because:

We think it's too restrictive

We think it means we can't have fun

We think it means we're "struggling"

Or we simply don't want to *look at the truth*

So instead, we do what most people do:

We *wing it.*

We spend off memory and feelings.
We keep numbers in our head instead of on paper.
We "think" we know what's left — until the card gets declined.

Then we sit there talking about:

"I don't know where all my money goes."

Yes you do.
It went exactly where you **sent it** —
you just didn't track the route.

The Real Reason Budgets Feel Hard

Most people think a budget is a **restriction.**

But a budget is actually **permission.**

It says:

You *can* spend on this.

You *will* enjoy this.

67

And you *won't* feel guilty while doing it.

A budget is not saying:
"You can't have it."

A budget is saying:
"You can have it — in the right order and at the right time."

What's Really Blocking Us

We don't avoid budgets because they're complicated.

We avoid budgets because **we don't want to face our truth.**

Because once the numbers are written down:

We can't pretend we're doing better than we are.

We can't lie to ourselves about what we can "afford."

We can't hide emotional spending behind
"treating myself."

The budget forces **accountability**.

And accountability forces **growth**.

And growth forces us to let go of who we were
—
so we can become who we were called to be.

And that…
is uncomfortable.

But discomfort is the doorway to freedom.

Budgets Don't Limit You. They *Position* You.

A budget is how you tell your money:

"You work for *me* now."

Because without a budget?
Your money is working for:

Restaurants

Car payments

Entertainment

Impulse decisions

Temporary feelings

Other people

But with a budget?
Your money starts building:

Savings

Investments

Cushion

Margin

Peace

Options

Options are wealth.

The wealthiest people in the world have one thing in common:

They know where their money is going — on purpose.

Here's the Reality

You don't need more income to change your life.
You need more **order**.

Because order stretches income.
Order multiplies income.
Order *protects* income.

Order is the difference between:

Constant stress
and

Constant progress.

So Here's the Practical Shift

A budget should be:

Simple enough to follow

Clear enough to see

Flexible enough to adjust

Honest enough to reveal your truth

Your budget isn't Excel.
It isn't categories.
It isn't receipts.

Your budget is your **future written down.**

And the moment you write it down —
your future stops living by accident and starts
being built **on purpose.**

Say This Out Loud:

**I don't budget because I'm broke.
I budget because my future matters.**

**I am becoming disciplined, structured, and
intentional.**

My money will reflect my purpose — not my impulses.

CHAPTER 9 — THE UPGRADE TRAP: "I DESERVE THIS" IS COSTING YOU YOUR FUTURE

Here's a moment we've all lived:

You've been working hard.
You've been pushing.
You've been tired.
You've been showing up for everybody.

Then you finally get a little extra money — maybe from:

Overtime

Tax season

A bonus

Side work

A new job

A refund

And the first thought that rises up is:

"I deserve something nice."

And listen — you *do*.

You deserve joy.
You deserve comfort.
You deserve to celebrate progress.

But here's the problem:

The world taught us to **celebrate stress relief, not progress.**

And that "little treat" mentality is how we stay stuck in the same financial place year after year.

Let's Tell the Truth

Most of us aren't "treating ourselves" because we're thriving.

75

We're treating ourselves because we're exhausted.

We are rewarding:

Overworking

Stress

Emotional burnout

Survival mode

And we call it:
"I earned this."

But what did we *actually* earn?

Relief.
Not progress.
Distraction.
Not development.

And relief is temporary.

Progress is permanent.

The Upgrade Trap Looks Like This:

You get a raise → you upgrade your apartment.

Your car starts working fine → you trade it in for something newer.

You get a better job → you start eating out more.

You get a little savings → you start "deserving" treats again.

Every time your income goes up…
your lifestyle goes up *with it*.

So your bank account stays the same.
Your stress stays the same.
Your lack of peace stays the same.

You're growing — but **your life isn't improving.**

Because all that changed were your *expenses*.

This Is Why So Many Hardworking People Stay Broke

Not because they don't make money.
They do.

But because every time life expands,
their spending expands **before their future does.**

We're living for the moment we can breathe...

...but the moment we catch our breath,
we start suffocating our future again.

Stop and feel that.

The Truth About "I Deserve It"

You *do* deserve things.

But you don't deserve:

Stress every payday

Sleepless nights worrying about bills

Anxiety when your card gets swiped

Shame when you can't cover an emergency

You deserve:

Peace

Margin

Options

Flexibility

Security

Rest that doesn't require running from
responsibility to feel better

Treating yourself is not the problem.

Treating yourself *instead of building yourself* is.

The Shift

We don't stop celebrating.

We just change *how* we celebrate.

Instead of:

New clothes

New gadgets

New car

New hairstyle every two weeks

Eating out "just because"

We celebrate with:

Extra payment toward debt

Money transferred to savings

Investment contribution

Emergency fund growth

Something that *pays us back later*

Because grown celebration is:

Not showing off today

But ensuring tomorrow feels safe.

Say This Out Loud:

My future deserves more than my impulses. I will not sabotage tomorrow for comfort today.

When I celebrate, I will celebrate growth — not escape.

CHAPTER 10 — INSURANCE: PROTECTING YOUR LIFE WHILE YOU BUILD IT

Let's have a grown conversation.

We work hard.
We sacrifice.
We grind.
We push.
We build plans and dream big.

But one emergency —
one accident —
one medical situation —
one unexpected event —

…can wipe out **years** of progress if we are not *covered.*

Insurance is not about fear.
Insurance is about **peace.**

Not just peace right now —
but peace in the storm.

Because storms don't schedule appointments.
They just show up.

Here's the Hard Truth

Most of us avoid insurance because:

It feels boring

It doesn't feel "urgent"

We think we can do it later

We think nothing will happen to us

But here's the problem:

Life doesn't ask for permission to change.

And when life changes without protection in
place…

we are forced to make decisions out of panic, not wisdom.

And panic is expensive.

Insurance Is Not a Bill — It's a Barrier

A barrier against:

Financial disaster

Medical debt

Legal issues

Family being left unprepared

A crisis turning into a setback

Insurance turns:
"What if?"
into
"Even if."

Even if something happens…

The kids are alright.

The house is alright.

The savings are intact.

The future is protected.

That is peace.

Let's Break Down the Essentials

There are four main types of insurance every household must have:

1. Life Insurance — For Your Family

If something happens to you, your children should not have to:

Start over

Be relocated

Depend on GoFundMe

Lose stability

You love your family too much to leave them unprepared.

This isn't about death.
It's about **legacy.**

2. Health Insurance — For Your Body and Sanity

Medical bills are the *#1 cause* of personal bankruptcy in America.

One ER visit can cost:

$3,000+ just to walk through the door

$12,000+ for a simple procedure

$40,000+ for something major

It is cheaper to be insured than to recover from a medical bill.

3. Renters or Homeowners Insurance — For Where You Live

Disasters don't ask if you're ready.

Whether you rent or own:

Insure your home.

Protect your belongings.

Have liability coverage in case anything happens on your property.

Small premiums.
Big peace.

4. Auto Insurance — For Reality

If you drive — you need real coverage.
Not the cheapest bare-minimum policy.

If something happens:

You want protection for the other car.

Protection for yourself.

Protection for your future.

Because one accident can turn into a lawsuit real quick —
and without coverage, **they can take your money, your savings, your tax return, even garnish your paycheck.**

We don't play with that.

This Is What Mature Wealth Looks Like

Not flashy.
Not loud.
Not for social media.
Not for validation.

Protection is grown.
Protection is wise.
Protection is love.

And love isn't just what we feel —
love is what we secure.

Say This Out Loud:

**My family will never struggle because I failed to plan.
I protect what I build. I protect who I love.**

My future will not be left to chance. It will be covered.

CHAPTER 11 — YOU CANNOT SAVE YOUR WAY INTO WEALTH

Let's talk elevation.

Because up until now, we've been focusing on:

Cutting costs

Reducing stress

Breaking habits

Shifting priorities

Rebuilding structure

But hear me clearly:

You cannot shrink yourself into financial freedom.
You must grow into it.

Cutting back gives you **breathing room.**
Increasing income gives you **power.**

Savings protects you.
Income **positions** you.

And positioning is where destiny moves.

Here's the Truth That Most People Never Learn

You can budget perfectly.
You can meal prep consistently.
You can lower your expenses and get your life in order...

...but if your income never increases,
your financial life will always have a ceiling.

You cannot build:

Wealth

Ownership

Legacy

Freedom

...off the same paycheck that was only designed to help you survive.

At some point, the **money coming in** has to grow.

But Let's Be Real

Most of us were raised to be:

Grateful

Humble

Content

"Not do too much"

"Not ask for too much"

And that turned into:

Staying in the same job too long

Being underpaid

Being overworked

Being undervalued

Being afraid to ask for more

Settling for "just enough"

We thought humility meant shrinking.

But humility never meant poverty.

Humility means:
I know who my Source is — so I don't have to pretend or perform.

And because God is the Source…
increase is always available.

So Let's Talk About Income — The Right Way

There are 3 types of income you must build:

1. Active Income (Your job or business)

This is the money you earn from working.

This is your **foundation**, not your forever.

2. Supplemental Income (Side streams)

This is the additional income you build intentionally.

This is your **freedom factor.**

3. Passive Income (Investing, ownership, automated systems)

This is the income that works even when you rest.

This is your **legacy.**

You don't build all 3 at once.
You build in **stages** — on purpose.

Stage 1: Fix the Leaks

Stop the overspending.

Break emotional purchases.

94

Reduce unnecessary lifestyle.

Get intentional.

You've already begun this.

Stage 2: Grow the Income

You have **gifts** that the marketplace pays for.

Let me say that again:

You already have what you need to increase your income — you just haven't monetized it yet.

Look at your life:

Can you teach something?

Can you do something with your hands?

Do you have a skill others struggle with?

Do you have experience others need?

Have you overcome something others are still fighting?

Because someone is willing to pay to learn what you take for granted.

Your income is inside your identity.

Stage 3: Multiply the Income

When the income rises:

You don't upgrade the apartment.

You don't upgrade the car.

You don't upgrade the lifestyle.

You **upgrade the investments.**

That's where the future expands.

Say This Out Loud:

I do not live to survive.
I live to build.

I will not stay in the same financial level out
of habit or fear.

My gifts are valuable. My skills are needed.
My future is calling.

CHAPTER 12 — YOU DON'T NEED LOTS OF STREAMS. YOU NEED THE RIGHT ONES.

There's a lot of noise out here.

Everybody online is talking about:

"Multiple streams of income"

"Seven income streams"

"Make passive money in your sleep"

"Get rich doing nothing"

And it sounds good…

But let's be honest:

Most people don't need **seven streams.**
Most people can't even manage *one* correctly yet.

The goal is not to have a bunch of income streams.

The goal is to have **the right income streams**, in the **right order**, that match your life, your skills, your capacity, and your purpose.

Because if your income streams are **confusing, stressful, time-consuming, or inconsistent**, you didn't build wealth…

You just built **exhaustion** with a fancy name.

Wealth Is Not Built By Doing Everything.

Wealth is built by doing:

One thing well

Then adding the next

Then adding the next

Mastery → Momentum → Multiplication.

Not chaos → pretending → burnout.

So How Do We Choose the Right Streams?

We choose income streams based on 3 things:

1. What You're Naturally Good At

If it drains you, it won't last.
If it fits you, it will *flow*.

Ask yourself:

What do people compliment me for?

What do others ask for my help with?

What feels natural to me?

There's income in that.

2. What the Market Pays For

Skills make money.
Personality makes connection.
Service makes income consistent.

Look around:

What problems do people keep having?

What do people keep needing?

What do people keep avoiding that you can do easily?

Solve that — and the money finds you.

3. What Fits Your Current Schedule

You don't need income that steals time from:

Your peace

Your family

Your rest

Your sanity

Your new income streams must **add**, not drain.

If it stresses you — it costs too much.

There Are Only 5 Real Categories of Income Streams

Everything else rolls under one of these:

Type	Example	Why It Matters
Work You Do	Job, Trade Skill, Coaching, Service Work	Reliable foundation
Skills You Sell	Workshops, Training, Digital Products, Tutoring	Scalable & flexible

Type	Example	Why It Matters
Things You Own	Property, Equipment Rentals, Cars on Turo	Passive with structure
Online Monetization	Content, Courses, Affiliate, Community	Compounding impact
Investments	Stocks, Index Funds, IRA/401k, Brokerage	Legacy + Long-term wealth

You don't build all five right away.

You build **one strong foundation,**
then **add one supplemental stream,**
then grow into **ownership/investing.**

Step by Step. Not all at once.

What Keeps Most People Stuck?

Trying to start 4 things at the same time with:

No focus

No plan

No consistency

No follow-through

That's not entrepreneurship.
That's **busy confusion.**

We are not building chaos.
We are building **order → stability → overflow.**

Here's the New Rule

If a new income idea does not increase peace and progress, it is not for this season.

Just because it's a good idea doesn't mean it's **your** idea.

Just because it works for them doesn't mean it fits **you.**

We are not chasing opportunity.
We are **strategically developing capacity.**

Say This Out Loud:

I don't need everything. I need what is aligned.
My income will grow with purpose, not panic.

I build wealth the same way I build faith —
consistently, patiently, intentionally.

105

CHAPTER 13 — DISCIPLINE: THE BRIDGE TO YOUR NEXT LEVEL

Let's talk about the part we don't always like to discuss.

Not money.
Not budgeting.
Not income.

Discipline.

Because every breakthrough you want —
financial, spiritual, emotional, relational —
is sitting on the other side of one thing:

Doing what needs to be done, even when you don't feel like doing it.

And let's be real:

Feelings are loud.
Comfort is persuasive.
Old habits feel familiar.

106

Growth is uncomfortable.

But discomfort is not your enemy.
Discomfort is **your training ground.**

We Have Been Conditioned to Chase Comfort

For years, we've used:

Spending to feel better

Shopping to feel valuable

Going out to escape stress

Food to calm anxiety

Entertainment to avoid thinking

Upgrades to validate our progress

But comfort has a silent cost:

It delays everything we say God promised us.

Comfort will have you:

Stuck in the same place

With the same paycheck

With the same habits

With the same stress

Calling it "normal"

But there is nothing normal about *struggling every month and calling it life.*

There is nothing normal about **survival being your default setting.**

Discipline Is Not Punishment.

Discipline is **alignment.**

It's saying:

"My future matters too much for me to keep living like this."

Discipline is how you tell your life:

Who's in charge

Where we're going

What we're not doing anymore

And what we're building now

Discipline is **self-respect in action.**

Your Future Needs More from You

Future you is:

Stable
Confident
Peaceful
Prepared
Strong
Focused
Free

Future you is not stressed.
Future you is not scattered.
Future you is not exhausted.

Future you is not running from the past —
Future you is running *toward destiny*.

But future you cannot exist...
until current you gets disciplined.

This Is Where Most People Quit

They start strong.
They get motivated.
They make a plan.

But when motivation fades —
they go right back to old patterns.

Because motivation is emotional.
Discipline is **spiritual.**

Motivation speaks to the moment.
Discipline speaks to the mission.

Motivation changes feelings.
Discipline changes identity.

How to Build Discipline (Even If You Never Had It Before)

Let's make this simple:

1. Make Your Decisions *Before* Life Happens

Don't decide in the moment.
Decide in advance.

"This is my grocery budget."

"This is my eating-out budget."

"This is my savings amount every check."

Once it's decided — it's done.

No negotiating with your temptations.

2. Create Structure That Doesn't Rely on Willpower

Willpower is inconsistent.
Systems are steady.

That means:

Automation

Scheduled transfers

Pre-set spending limits

Visual budgets

Written reminders

Structure makes discipline **automatic.**

3. Keep Promises to Yourself

Every time you tell yourself you're going to do something — and you don't — you teach your mind not to trust you.

But every time you follow through — even a small thing — you build **strength.**

Self-trust = self-discipline.

Say This Out Loud:

I am not who I used to be. I am becoming who I was created to be.

My discipline is my declaration.
My consistency is my breakthrough.

I am worth the work.
My future is worth the sacrifice.
My life will reflect my purpose.

CHAPTER 14 — PEACE: THE REAL MEASURE OF WEALTH

Let's take a breath here.

Not the shallow breath we take when we're rushing.
Not the tired breath we take when we're overwhelmed.
A real breath.

Because peace is not just silence.
Peace is not just paying bills on time.
Peace is not just having a few dollars saved.

Peace is the quiet confidence that you are no longer living in survival mode.

Peace is:

Not flinching when your phone rings.

Not holding your breath when your card is swiped.

114

Not praying your car makes it another 30 miles.

Not panicking when a bill comes early.

Not depending on hope to make it through the month.

Peace is:
Your life being stable, structured, and supported — from the inside out.

Peace Is Not Passive. Peace Is Built.

Peace is the result of:

Discipline

Boundaries

Intention

Structure

Honesty

Consistency

Peace is what happens when your decisions align with your future.

Peace is what happens when you stop running.

Peace is what happens when you stop pretending.

We Used to Think Peace Was a Moment

A vacation.
A massage.
A brunch outing.
A weekend away.
A hotel night to escape.

But peace that requires escaping your own life is not peace.

That's *relief.*

Relief feels good.
But relief fades.

Peace *remains*.

Peace Shows Up Quietly

You'll know you're healing financially when:

Payday doesn't feel like rescue anymore.

Eating out is a choice, not a coping mechanism.

Bills are handled before they're due.

Emergency funds exist *before* emergencies.

You don't have to "treat yourself" to prove you're okay.

Your lifestyle grows slower than your income.

You can say "no" without guilt.

You're not afraid to check your bank account.

That's peace.

And it's priceless.

Peace Also Changes Your Presence

Your voice becomes calmer.
Your mind becomes clearer.
Your decisions become stronger.
Your relationships feel lighter.
Your confidence stops needing validation.

Because peace is **internal wealth.**

The world can't give it.
And the world can't take it away.

But This Is the Most Important Part

Peace is not the *end goal.*

Peace is the **environment** where your purpose grows.

118

When your mind is quiet — you can hear God's direction.
When your schedule isn't frantic — you can move with intention.
When your finances aren't chaotic — you can build something real.

Peace is not the finish line.
Peace is the **foundation.**

Say This Out Loud:

**Peace is my new normal.
Chaos is not my portion.**

My life is settling. My mind is clear. My future is stable.

I do not chase peace. I create it. I protect it. I live in it.

CHAPTER 15 — LEGACY: YOUR NAME IS SUPPOSED TO MEAN SOMETHING

Let's be very clear:

All of this —
the budgeting, the discipline, the sacrifices, the mindset shifts, the financial restructuring —

was never just about money.

This has always been about **your name.**
Your lineage.
Your bloodline.
Your story.
Your children's children.
Your future grandchildren who haven't even taken their first breath yet.

This has always been about **legacy.**

Legacy is not what you *leave behind when you die*.
Legacy is what you *set in motion while you're alive*.

Legacy Starts With the Decision to Break What Broke You

You are the one who said:

"The struggle stops with me."

"The chaos ends here."

"My kids will not repeat what I had to recover from."

"My grandchildren will know abundance as their normal."

"We will not pass down survival anymore."

That decision alone is **historic**.

You are not just changing your life —
you are changing **your bloodline's future.**

And I need you to feel the weight of that…
not as pressure, but as **purpose.**

Your Story Does Not End With What You Survived

You've survived:

Setbacks

Lack

Mistakes

Delays

Disappointments

Restart after restart

And yet — you are still here.

Not just alive…
Awake.

Awake enough to say:

"I'm ready to build something that lasts."

That's legacy.

Legacy Has Four Pillars

To build something that outlives you, you must establish:

Alignment — Who are you? What do you stand for?

Instruction — What do you teach your children about money, discipline, identity, faith?

Protection — Insurance, savings, documents, wills, financial strategy.

Transfer — Assets, information, habits, values, and opportunities.

Legacy is not just:

> Wealth

Property

Businesses

Investments

Legacy is:

Wisdom

Emotional health

Financial stability

A spiritual foundation

A mindset that says **"We do not break. We build."**

Your Children Need Your Healed Leadership

Not your perfection.
Not your riches.
Not your guilt.

They need:

- Your consistency
- Your example
- Your standards
- Your correction rooted in love
- Your belief in them
- Your blueprint

They are watching **how you live**, not just what you say.

And your transformation gives them permission to transform sooner than you did.

They get to start where you *finish*.

That is legacy.

Your Name Will Be Spoken Differently After This

Right now, there may be:

125

Struggle in your history

Debt in your history

Chaos in your history

Financial instability in your history

But that is **history.**

You are writing the chapter where your name
becomes:

- Strong
- Strategic
- Respected
- Stable
- Protective
- Generational

Your grandchildren will say:

**"We never struggled because of the work *they*
did."**

Your great-grandchildren will say:

"We have opportunities because of the decisions *they* made."

Your name will not be remembered for survival.

Your name will be remembered for establishment.

Say This Out Loud:

My family will eat because I decided to change.
My lineage will rise because I refused to quit.

The struggle ends with me.
Legacy begins with me.
This is the chapter where my name becomes foundation.

CHAPTER 16 — THE NEW YOU: WALKING IN YOUR FUTURE

Let's pause for a moment.

Not to reflect on where you've been —
but to acknowledge who you've become.

Because you are **not** the same person who started this journey.

You are:

- More aware
- More intentional
- More grounded
- More disciplined
- More confident
- More focused
- More aligned with your purpose

And most importantly…

You are **awake.**

Awake to your patterns.
Awake to your habits.
Awake to your identity.
Awake to your calling.
Awake to your financial reality.
Awake to your power.

This is not a phase.
This is not temporary.
This is **transformation.**

You Are Not "Trying" Anymore.

Trying is passive.
Trying is emotional.
Trying allows quitting.

You're not "trying to get better with money."
You're **doing it.**

You're budgeting.

You're planning.

You're structuring.

You're making decisions on purpose.

You're saying no when necessary.

You're choosing your future over impulse.

You're prioritizing peace over performance.

This isn't effort.

This is identity.

This Is Who You Are Now

You are someone who:

Protects your peace

Manages money with honor

Invests in your future

Builds with intention

Speaks life into your household

Models discipline with grace

Walks with purpose in your steps

Loves yourself enough to grow

Loves your family enough to change

Loves your future enough to plan ahead

You are no longer:

- Surviving
- Scrambling
- Chasing relief
- Running from your finances
- Hiding from the truth

You are walking in clarity.

And clarity is power.

You Are Allowed to Celebrate Yourself

Not because you are finished —
but because you finally **started.**

And starting is what changes everything.

This is not the end of the journey.
This is the **activation of a new standard.**

A standard that says:

"I honor my life."

"I honor my purpose."

"I honor my family."

"I honor my legacy."

And I do it through discipline, structure, and peace.

Say This Out Loud:

Take your time. Let it sink in.

I am not who I was. I am who I am becoming.
My life is shifting. My mind is clear. My habits are aligned.

Peace is my home now.
Wisdom is my strategy.
Discipline is my lifestyle.

I build on purpose.
I grow on purpose.
I succeed on purpose.

My name will mean something.
And my life will reflect what I was created for.

This Is Your New Starting Point

Not the end of the book.
The beginning of your new life.

Every step from here is:

- Intentional

- Strategic
- Peaceful
- Aligned
- Purpose-driven

Welcome to the new you.

A you that builds more than they consume.
A you that creates more than they crave.
A you that leads more than they follow.
A you that leaves **legacy**, not just memories.

You are becoming the person your future needs.

And your future is smiling back at you.

Other Books by Rev. Darryl Bass

Your Money Isn't the Problem, Your Mindset Is

A transformational work that challenges limiting financial beliefs and redefines wealth from the inside out, empowering readers to align their identity with abundance and responsibility.

This Is Why You're Broke

A bold and unapologetic examination of the habits, beliefs, and financial behaviors that keep people trapped in cycles of struggle. This book confronts uncomfortable truths and replaces excuses with execution, helping readers shift from reactive spending to strategic wealth building.

The Financial Identity Shift

A mindset-and-behavior reset that helps readers align who they are with how they handle money, transforming financial habits through identity-based discipline.

The Life Progression System

A comprehensive blueprint for intentional living, The Life Progression System guides readers through structured personal growth, goal alignment, mindset transformation, and legacy building. It equips individuals with practical tools to move from drifting through life to deliberately designing it.

The Life Progression System Workbook

A companion workbook to the Life Progression System book that allows readers to progress through various tasks, exercises and assignments as they learn.

Financial Progression System

This book provides a step-by-step roadmap to financial stability and long-term wealth building. It teaches readers how to increase income, eliminate debt, build credit, create savings systems, and establish generational financial security.

Borrowed Futures

A wake-up call about the hidden costs of debt and financial shortcuts, showing readers how to escape debt cycles and build futures without financial bondage.

Life Insurance: The Gift of Life After Life

More than a policy explanation, this book reframes life insurance as a strategic wealth-building and legacy-protection tool. It educates families on how to use life insurance for income replacement, debt protection, estate planning, generational wealth transfer, and financial leverage.

The Intellectual Property Wealth Blueprint

A strategic guide to turning knowledge into income, this book teaches creators how to package ideas into books, courses, systems, and assets that generate scalable and recurring revenue streams.

The Intellectual Property Wealth Blueprint 2.0

Focused on licensing, certification, and legacy systems, this volume expands intellectual property into scalable enterprises that create long-term wealth and generational ownership structures.

Coming Soon!

The Overcomer's Wealth Plan

A resilient strategy guide for those rising from adversity, this book outlines disciplined financial recovery, structured planning, and long-term legacy development.

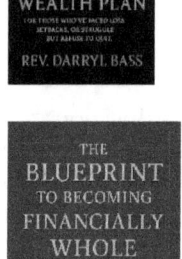

The Blueprint to Becoming Financially Whole

A holistic financial transformation guide that goes beyond budgeting and debt elimination. This book teaches readers how to align mindset, money management, protection strategies, income growth, and legacy planning into one cohesive financial structure built for stability and abundance.

Stewards of Legacy

A leadership and responsibility manifesto focused on generational impact. This book challenges readers to move beyond consumption and become builders—individuals who protect, multiply, and transfer wealth, wisdom, and values to future generations.

The Debt Eliminator

Coming 2026

What if 2026 was the year everything changed?

What if this was the year you stopped surviving... and started building?
The year you stopped juggling bills... and started creating wealth?
The year debt stopped controlling your decisions?

The **Debt Eliminator** is not another budgeting class. It is a structured financial transformation system designed to help individuals and families break free from consumer debt, rebuild financial confidence, and establish a foundation for long-term wealth.

This course was built for hardworking people who are tired of living paycheck to paycheck. It was created for families who want stability, not stress. It was designed for individuals who know they are capable of more— but need a system that works.

What the Debt Eliminator Will Teach You:

• How to eliminate consumer debt strategically and aggressively
• How to increase income without adding overwhelm
• How to rebuild and optimize your credit profile
• How to build savings while eliminating debt
• How to structure emergency funds and protection plans
• How to shift your financial identity from borrower to builder
• How to create systems that prevent debt from returning

This is not theory.
This is execution.

Through step-by-step modules, implementation tools, accountability structure, and real-life application, you will learn how to take control of your money instead of letting it control you.

Imagine waking up without financial anxiety.
Imagine having a plan.
Imagine watching your balances decrease and your confidence increase.
Imagine positioning your household for ownership, investing, and generational legacy.

That transformation begins in 2026.

The Debt Eliminator is more than a course.
It is a movement toward financial clarity, discipline, and freedom.

Get ready to break cycles.
Get ready to build stability.
Get ready to eliminate debt—permanently.

The Debt Eliminator — Launching 2026.

Join our waiting list Today!
https://savingssolution.org/join

The Financial Freedom Revolution Tour

Launching 2026

This is not a seminar.
This is not a motivational rally.
This is a financial awakening.

The **Financial Freedom Revolution Tour** is a live, high-impact experience designed to ignite transformation in individuals, families, entrepreneurs, and communities ready to break financial cycles and build generational stability.

For too long, people have been working harder but falling further behind. Income rises. Expenses rise. Stress rises. Yet true financial progress feels out of reach.

The Revolution changes that.

This national tour brings together powerful teaching, real strategy, live coaching, and structured execution

plans that move attendees from confusion to clarity—
and from debt to disciplined wealth-building.

What You'll Experience:

• A clear roadmap to financial stability and long-term
wealth
• Step-by-step strategies for eliminating consumer debt
• Income growth frameworks and entrepreneurship
positioning
• Credit optimization and financial leverage strategies
• Protection planning and legacy-building principles
• Live financial assessments and actionable
implementation steps
• A mindset shift from survival thinking to ownership
thinking

This is not inspiration without structure.
This is strategy with accountability.

The Financial Freedom Revolution Tour is built for
families who want peace instead of pressure. For
entrepreneurs who want profit with structure. For

leaders who understand that financial stability is the foundation for community impact.

Imagine thousands gathered in one space—learning, planning, committing to real change.
Imagine leaving with a clear blueprint instead of just excitement.
Imagine knowing exactly what steps to take the next day.

This is more than an event.
It is a declaration that debt cycles end here.
It is a call to financial responsibility, ownership, and generational leadership.

Cities across the country will host this movement in 2026.

Seats will fill.
Lives will shift.
Legacies will be built.

The Financial Freedom Revolution Tour — Coming 2026.

This is the year you stop reacting to money
…and start commanding it.

The revolution begins with one decision.

https://savingssolution.org/tour

Follow on Social Media

Facebook

https://www.facebook.com/LPSCoach

Twitter

https://twitter.com/LPS_Coach

Instagram

https://www.instagram.com/lps_coach/

YouTube

https://www.youtube.com/@life_progressio
n_system

TikTok

https://www.tiktok.com/@debt_annihilator

LinkedIn

https://www.linkedin.com/in/lpscoach/

www.ingramcontent.com/pod-product-compliance
Lightning Source LLC
Chambersburg PA
CBHW071309220526
45468CB00001B/307